From T

Mark Greenlaw

Contents

From The Ashes Prologue

The Phoenix is a flaming bird associated with rebirth and a losing of one's old self. Originally this poetry collection was created with the themes *The Good, The Bad, and The Ugly*. I have renamed the collection to *From the Ashes* as it represents the loss of all the negative events, feelings, people, and hurts from my childhood. As such I have kept *The Good, The Bad, and The Ugly* as sections instead of individual collections; hence the Phoenix rising from the ashes is symbolic of the new me emerging amid the chaos of my life.

What to expect from these writings: to be honest they are just writings I have done as the mood has stricken. I am a survivor of emotional, physical, and sexual abuse, as well as neglect. *The Good* section is just a collection of poetry I have written that are positive, light hearted and maybe a little funny. *The Bad* and *The Ugly* are events or feelings from when I was navigating through it all. I organized them as I felt in regards to the difficulty of me dealing with them as I wrote them. The worse I felt afterwards, or if the emotions were strong, then they were put into *The Ugly* section.

I am a baptized Christian who is learning how to become a better dad, and husband and follower of Christ. I attend *Celebrate Recovery* (CR) and have been for 4 years. I hope these writings will help you navigate through whatever you are as a survivor from, or perhaps even still going through, as you are reading this.

A final note on my poetry; I believe poetry should be free form. I don't use Iambic Pentameter or follow any rhyme scheme. I write from the heart, mind, and soul, and follow nothing else. I hope you enjoy some of these and maybe those of you that share a similar experience and can relate.

Be Blessed –

Mark Greenlaw

The Good

From the Ashes

When I think about all my childhood memories the pain and sadness is often too much to bear.

It is a story of bravery and abuse and scenarios that are a complete nightmare.

From emotional, sexual and physical abuse and neglect that boggle the mind.

I had 2 brothers to help me and a Mom that was strong; supportive and kind.

I also had the one and only true God help me to rise above it all.

Like the fiery Phoenix from the ashes; like leaves on the ground in the fall.

A lot of times the cycle of abuse will continue from person to the rest.

But I have ended them all with me, I had passed life's battle test.

Jesus was my Shepard through the tears, the abuse and pain.

I found my strength in his word; over everything God does reign.

As the Phoenix soars high in the sky leaving ashes in its wake.

I have myself been reborn, my old sins left behind with a final shake.

I have learned how to trust in God and everything I do.

My past is left behind like a worn-out old shoe.

I look ahead to the future now as a full-grown new man.

I live my life now for His Purpose; the best that I can.

Like the Phoenix; from the ashes I have risen.

Newly made, forgiveness found, in peaceful precision.

The past is just life's way to teach us a lesson.

Remember God, use his strength, he will get you through. You will get his blessing.

Eyes

When those eyes stare at me they take me to
another place.

They are by far the best feature on the
woman's face.

Filled with intrigue, and desire they are very
captivating.

I helplessly look. What I see is very
fascinating.

Sometimes they can express the very depth
of a woman's sadness.

But just hold her, hug, and the eyes will
glimmer her gladness.

Like a bed of rose petals, they can be
sensuous, soft and sweet.

A woman's eyes quite simply, will sweep me
off my feet.

Like an on-coming storm they can narrow into pictures of rage.

When this look you get; do not in combat; ENGAGE!

A body part beyond compares; as limitless as the skies.

It is the incredible, unbelievable, part of a woman. Her EYES!

Seasons Haiku

Spring brings about much joy and happiness with
every flower that shows color.

With coming snow there
is the cold that follows and laughter of children.

The BEE

Yesterday I saw a BEE!

It looked at me and I at him.

He buzzed around from flower to flower.

Before long I realized I had watched for an hour.

He paid no attention to little ole me.

For there was no threat that he could see.

I was of no importance he clearly thought.

The thought of this made me boiling hot.

Doesn't he know that I am a human?

Away from me now he ought to be zoomin'!

With haughty steps I yelled "BEWARE!"

I swung and I swung but I struck only air.

He zigged and he zagged, and he kept me guessing.

And then he decided to teach me a lesson.

He zoomed right in and stung my knee.

Thus! Teaching me.... HUMILITY.

The Cross

I am the one that made the sacrifice.

Awe inspired by my mighty father and king who gave life to all and who simply asks that we worship him in all that we do.

His beauty, wisdom, power and grace should inspire us to do what is right.

My sacrifice is the biggest sacrifice the world has ever seen.

I have given so many sermons, prayers, miracles, and life to all those who have arrived and believe in us.

I love you

Jesus Christ

The Owl

It was a warm summer night out deep in the woods.

I lay in my tent next to my camping goods. "It's pretty cozy here with no kid and no wife." Just as I try to sleep the forest comes to life.

There's a chorus of crickets, frogs, and other noises too. But from somewhere nearby I hear a loud "Who? Who?" I try counting sheep two by two.

But it's hard counting sheep when you keep hearing "Who? Who?"

I race to the noise raising quite a commotion.

What's making the noise? I haven't a notion.

I stop and I listen for a minute or two.

Alas! I hear it! "Who? Who?"

I look intently up the tree.

Two big yellow eyes stare down at me.

My laughter starts small but ends in a howl.

"This noise is being made by a silly ole owl"

"Stop Who-ing at me! I need to sleep!" When I yelled these words, I didn't hear a peep.

As I walked away my smile of victory grew.

It vanished quickly when again I heard "Who?

Who?"

In frustration I started to shake the tree.

But un-concerned the owl stared down at me.

"Who gave you the right to keep me up all night?"

"Who? Who?" was its only response.

"Who created you to be such a pest?"

"Who created you to give me no rest?"

"Who? Who?" the owl repeated.

When it again says "Who? Who?" I started to think.

When the answer hit me, the owl gave me a wink.
"If God made the owl go "Who? Who?" then he made me act stupid too."

These thoughts crept into my tired head.
"I can blame someone else then go to bed." Then without so much as a second thought.
I gave the owl my parting shot.

"Well, who is that made me act so lame?"

"Tell me! Tell me! Who's to blame?"

The owl read my thoughts and knew what I was trying to do.

He stunned me when he answered "You! You!"

With my head hung low I head back to my tent.

My mind is exhausted. It is totally spent.

The dark pit of loneliness creeps back into my life.

I wish I had company. My kid, and my wife.

The Parts of a Woman

The Hair of a woman smells fresh, like a fully
opened rose.
Whether long or short, it adds to her beauty; and it
shows.
It likes to be tussled, teased, and have fingers
running through it.
With elegance and style, it gives the woman true
merit.

The Eyes of a woman are like a mysterious,
winding forest.
You can get lost in them for hours, never tiring;
staring at beauty in its purest.
They twinkle, they shine, they glare, and they
wink.
This part of the women is the most attractive, I
THINK!

The touch of a woman provides intense pleasure.
With a caress, as delicate as a butterfly's wing.
OOOOH! What a treasure!
The hands feel nice when you are holding them on the beach.
Or when in the heat of passion; in the dark; the hands do reach....

The heart of a woman is like a complex puzzle.
But it holds all their secrets, it's what men should nuzzle.
Remember, Gentlemen! How fragile and delicate the women are.
Treat them with respect, and dignity, you'll get more from them by far.
Their heart just wants to be safe, happy, and filled with love.
There is nothing better in this world, then the women we love!!

The Soapbox Speech

Here I stand on my soapbox, ready to spew and spout.

There's a problem with the human race that I want to speak about.

They portray "A look, a trend, a fashion" as something beautiful.

They disregard the soul of a person, and that is pitiful.

Beauty consists of many things not just a "pretty face".

Like kindness, sincerity, and trust; qualities you can't replace.

A touch, a smell, and a smile make a person so valuable.

Not any of that cosmetic silicone junk that makes your body malleable.

Tenderness of heart, and purity of soul. Things a beautiful person contains.

Not vanity, fame, or glamour as the advertiser claims.

Beauty comes in many shapes, colors, and sizes.

But if you aren't a "perfect ten!" Why is you that society despises? What is the world coming to where people are so vain?

Don't they realize that in ignorance, they are causing so much pain? Here I stand shaking my finger at the people who are so blind.

Beauty is everywhere, in every person, just open your dumb mind.

Beauty is the creation of a child.

Beauty is staring at the creatures of the wild.

Beauty is in every place.

Beauty is in every face.

Beauty is found in every body part.

Beauty is found by those with a HEART.

Mark steps off his soapbox with tears in his eyes.

I Am

Probing your heart is what I do best.
Each and every time you pass the test.
Sometimes you laugh. Sometimes you cry.
At times like this, you know I'll be by.

I ensnare you in my warm, warm arms.
You know full well, I mean no harm.
And once, you're in my very firm grasp.
It seems like time will never elapse.

I am what cause the joy, the laughter.
I serve it all on a never-ending platter.
And as you savor, devour, and relish this savory treat.
There's no way in the world. You'll ever know defeat.

So, sit back, relax, and enjoy what I offer.
For I do it so willingly. I want not a copper.
Materialistic things, I want not a part.
All that matters; is what's in the heart.

Dreadfully; so dreadfully; when you pass away.
I'll still be with you; I'm here to stay. It'll be like a never-ending courtship.
You know who I am. For I am FRIENDSHIP

This poem I created for a patient when she knew she was dying. She wanted me to write this for her husband.

Carl

We've been together now for seventeen wonderful years.

You've been my stronghold, protecting me from all my fears.

My heart is bursting at the seams at how great you make me feel.

I am so in love with you it all just seems so surreal.

Carl you've been my side all the times I've needed you the most.

You're the best husband in the world, this poem is sure to boast.

You've grabbed my heart, mind, and completely overtaken my soul.

The minute you walk into the room, my life just feels so whole.

My love for you is so strong it will never, ever subside.

I know I can defeat anything with you right by my side.

You mean the world to me I love you beyond compare.

There is no-one else in this world who my life I wish to share.

Carl, you have blessed me with all that awesome things you do.

I want to express from every section of my heart;

I Love You! I Love You! I Love You!

With eternal love,

Betsy

They Call This Grace

John 1:16 NIV

"Out of his fullness we have all received grace in place of grace already given."

It starts with the Gift from the Almighty One.

A heavenly life for us; his sacrificial Son.

What he did on that cross cannot be undone.

The war for us; the war for us he won….

Chorus:

He saved the human race, through pain and

disgrace,

They call this Grace, They call this grace.

His sacrifice for us cannot be replaced

They call this grace… They call this grace….

It is a father's love; when the prodigal son returns.

It's when the woman at the well for acceptance yearns.

It is through heartache and loss; a price too heavy a cost.

When you see it through; when you pick up your cross…..

Chorus:

He saved the human race, through pain and

disgrace,

They call this Grace, They call this grace.

His sacrifice for us cannot be replaced

They call this grace… They call this grace….

It is when we are poor and yet our food we share.

When he loves us even when we don't seem to care.

To find grace; Jesus is the first place you start!

Can you see it within your own heart?

Chorus:

He saved the human race, through pain and

disgrace,

They call this Grace, They call this grace.

His sacrifice for us cannot be replaced

They call this grace… They call this grace….

When you are hurting and crying tears like rain;

When you can't see beyond the pain.

Let Jesus take you into his embrace; his embrace

Receive his grace; receive his grace; receive his grace…

Chorus:

He saved the human race, through pain and disgrace,

They call this Grace, They call this grace.

His sacrifice for us cannot be replaced

They call this grace… They call this grace….

Chorus:

He saved the human race, through pain and disgrace,

They call this Grace, They call this grace.

His sacrifice for us cannot be replaced

They call this grace… They call this grace….
Repeat last line 4 times

This was written on Mother's Day 2022 when my mom was in hospital.

MOM

Not everyone can see or know all you've done to keep us kids alive.

You kissed all our boo-boos, and put band aids on our scrapes.

Above all; you kept us safe from HIM.

Mom you've withstood so much to protect us, I will never stop loving you.

You're the strongest woman I know, I am proud to call you MOM.

I remember as young boy when you tucked us in at night with the words "This little piggy…"

I just want you to know you did the best you could in the situation we were all in.

You always believed in me. That belief made me have a positive attitude about myself no matter what happened.

As a result of your belief in me I have become a great dad, and husband and an author.

From the bottom of my heart; thank you for being my mom.

I love you more than these words can convey.

I love you! I love you! I love you!

Love Mark

The Bad

How could you destroy my heart?

Of all the questions I have to ask this one contains the most important answer. I was under the crazy opinion that women wanted a man that could take care of them; to cry with them; to hold them; to stick with them through all the difficult times, but yet you took my naïve and trusting heart and fed it to the hungry wolves.

They devoured it whole, destroyed it leaving nothing but the blood on their lips. I am totally at a loss. I was working three jobs, while you claimed you had issues, and yet I was willing to stick through it with you. I went to all the parent teacher conferences with your daughter while you stayed at home sleeping. What kind of a parent does that make you? That's fine you were too tired to go, luckily for you I love your daughter too much to not make a showing, and still "in sickness and in health" I was true to you.

Even after my exhausting days at work there was housework to be done, supper to make, a child to play with, and which one of those did you partake in? What? I can't hear you! Speak up, oh you said none, I see. It is ok I understand you are going through your depression but you have pills for those, and quite frankly you aren't even making any sort of effort to attempt to help. So, you sleep all day, then you trash the house, and sit at the computer instant messaging your online friends and telling them what a sap you have for a husband.

I tell you over and over how I love you, and how things will be fine, but perhaps my rosy glasses were on a little too much. I come home from my jobs and it is your cue to make sure that I stay home to watch your daughter while you go to the bar drinking with your friends, in a simply platonic way. Part of me really believes you because let's be frank, you don't shower much, and you don't take care of yourself, and I lump it all as part of your "depression". I caught you once having cyber-sex and informed you that that was cheating, you said you understood then on my birthday

I am told you did sexual acts with an ex-boyfriend. Besides the ultimate disgust, and the freaky way he got off on watching you urinate, my heart is devastated.

I put in eight and half years for nothing but a lie. Like a fool I think about forgiving you, but as I told you it was only because my stepdaughter would've gotten crushed. Inevitably, you seal the deal by not cutting off your contact with your ex. I decide to leave the state of Maine and get a divorce and despite the fact that you told everyone that I was somehow at fault, which never worked because all of your friends said I should have divorced you years ago; I am finally free of you, and yet loneliness for my stepdaughter tug at the shattered pieces. The final straw I get to find out is that you have been have providing oral pleasures to people around town; during the marriage.

Unfortunately, for you despite the pain, and emotional roller coaster of the divorce I have an indomitable will and strong sense of character and refuse to let you bring me down into your quagmire of depression.

My heart was destroyed, and eaten by the wolves, but thanks to a new woman in my life, my heart became newly formed.

This poem was written for my Cousin Nancy Price for a moment when she needed it the most.

Remember When

Remember when you first saw her; so tiny, cute, and bright.
She always made you laugh. She filled you with delight.

Remember when she looked at you,
with her beady eyes, her nose, and tail.
And don't forget her pink little tongue; it'd be sure to cheer you up, without fail.

Remember when she played;
she was so fast and carefree.
When she was done, you'd scoop her up;
And hold her in your arms, oh so gently.

Remember when you by each other's side; through the good times and the bad. It is this kind of shared love; that made you both so glad.

Remember when you were both at the beach.

Remember when you were always within reach.

Remember when she hogged all of your bed.

Remember when she begged to be fed.

Remember when she passes away.

A place in your heart she will always stay. When loneliness tries to hit you now and then; just read this poem and.......

Remember when In loving Memory of Muffin Price.

I wrote this poem for a friend of mine who had lost her sister. I gathered information from her and this is what I created.

Sister

I know you were five years older but it doesn't make things hurt any less. I feel the sadness creeping in and I start to cry, I'm a mess.

It is then that I think about the wonderful times we shared, and how terrific a sister you were to me.

Memories of walking the beach together we were just happy as can be. A smile comes across my face, these memories just won't erase.

Remember, sis when we rode the horses, I was laughing as the wind blew on my face.

I feel the tears still coming on, but laughter is
holding on a mixture of emotions I now have.
Sis, you made those giant peanut butter cookies for
my birthday that memory still makes me laugh.
We walked through the street of Spain, a beautiful
time won't you agree?
On those streets of Mallorac we just had to stop to
have croissants and white coffee.
These memories make me smile; the tears recede
but let's be realistic for I am no fool.
They will return but for now I remember you
taking me to school in your jeep; that was so cool.
I choke back the tears remembering those coronas
and pizza we used to chase away the gloom.

We laughed so hard we almost choked; the nurses came running into the room.

I hold onto the fond memories of how you were such an amazing mom.

Muffin you were so creative, sewing, painting, or writing with such aplomb.

Organization was one of your strengths, and you were so full of intelligence and grace.

Your generosity held no bounds if you could you would give to the entire human race.

Some people put forth such minimum effort in all that they do. Steadfast, dedicated, and hardworking why can't more people be more like you?

I know I'll those times of grief, and cry like there is no relief;

But then there are these times, which fill me with such belief.

Belief that you are in wonderful place, my memories will always warm me through and through.

I miss you and think of you but most of all I love you.

The Boy Who Became King

The little boy lived his life in his world of writing and reading.

It kept him safe, oblivious to the mental and physical beatings.

His heart was wrapped tight around a steadfast and stubborn will.

He has remained himself through it all despite everything still.

A devilish smile dances across his thinking lips.

Smiling about a memory playing back like old movie clips.

It was supposed to be a tyrant's chance to show he was the "King"

The man became weakened the minute the BOY stepped into the ring.

It was cold and snowy, with many inches on the ground.

As a means to get the boys out of his sight, a chore had to be found.

"Go outside and shovel" he barked like a tiny yippy dog.

One brother put on his boots, but the boy stood as still as a log.

You see my mind and body was tired of being pushed around.

All these years of trying to break my will have failed. I stood my ground.

As I stand there defiantly un-moving, he seems to let out a hiss.

"What are you waiting for?" he asks. My response "Christmas!"

He ran across the room in a fit of rage.

I pushed a button. I rattled his cage.

He hauls back and hits the soft spot on the top of my head.

Unfazed, I stare back at him with eyes wishing him dead.

Seeing no fear in me he hits me twice more.

He is enraged at my lack of emotion, angry to the core.

It is the sight of rage so purple being displayed on his ugly face.

That is when to my side my brother did race.

He grabbed me, moved me to where my boots were.

He tells me later he was afraid about what was going to occur.

I know with every fiber of my being that I had on that day I won.

The man knew from that day on, no damage to me could be done.

It was a standoff, a battle, and to the victor my honest, and good heart.

I kept it, I preserved it, and now we will never part.

I'll cherish that memory and savor it for as long as I live.

That one simple lesson to the dethroned king; I did give.

The Cheat

The flood of tears spoke from my shattered,
hurting heart.
What possessed you to do such a thing? Have we
grown that far apart?

I left my heart into your hands; to be safe, loved,
and true.
Instead, it got thrown to the ground, by an act you
weren't supposed to do.

I'm devastated, confused, angry, and feel totally
alone.
I am shivering with sadness; it's shaking every
bone.

Our sacred vows, I'VE kept for eight plus years.
Gone by your selfish act; leaving me with many
fears.

Although I've said the words "FORGIVE" I find it hard to trust.
My tears are falling very hard. My dented suit might rust.

Many thoughts go whirling in my mind; thoughts of me and you. Where do we go from here? What am I supposed to do?

This is one of the few poems that is not a part of my life. Just a poem I wrote with a Shakespearean twist. I hope you enjoy!

The Phone Call

The night was full of thunder and rain.
Her heart was lonely; and searching in vain.
It was searching for the right man to fulfill her every need.
Then she found Him. From Loneliness' grasp; her heart was freed.
She remembers where they met, in a shop, near the beach.
His handsome features, deep voice, and the way his eyes seemed to reach.
Into her soul, they would penetrate; reaching to her inner core.
They talked. He was nice, and polite, then she noticed the ring he wore. As friends they

exchange numbers, but with sorrowful dread, she dismissed him from her mind.
Her phone rang one day. It was him. Her heart beat. "He's married" it tried to remind.
A stirring in her heart causes her to agree.
And the daring couple go out to a dinner and a movie.
After the movie he changed circumstance.
"C'mon! C'mon! The night's young. Let's dance!"
Her head is spinning, body's yearning, she wished on the stars above.
"Please! Please! Let this be my chance for love."
He made promises he did not think he would be able to keep.
Tears of joy; of happiness, she does weep.
It's a roller coaster of love that should not be.
Blinded by emotion, she does not see.
The crack of thunder breaks into her wonderful memory.

In the blink of an eye; her hopes died. She starts to recall painfully.

"I am sorry" he said. "I just can't leave my wife."

With a tear-stained face she replied. "How much longer am I to endure this life?" He made one final statement that she desperately holds onto; like a moth to a light. "If I end it with my wife, I will give you a call by nine o'clock tonight." With haggard eyes she watches the minutes tick.

"8:55" The hands tell her. "8:56" The hand moves one click.

The storm outside rages; and she stands up nervously to pace.

Sweat arrives and cascades down her beautiful face.

The woman gets up to get a drink of water, to calm her nerves.

With shaking hands, she drinks. Bravely, she summons up the last of her emotional reserves.

As the lightning flashes, she sees the clock.

"It's almost time!" She realizes in shock.
"The phone is in the living room". She realizes too late. "If he should call, I don't want him to wait."
Her love-crazed mind causes her to break into a dash.
She slips. She falls. There is a loud crash.
Through the glass coffee table, she falls face first.
A shard of glass hits her throat, where blood begins to spurt.
Feeling woozy and hurt she can feel the blood drain.
While outside there is the pitter-patter of uncaring rain.
"Oh, what trouble this thing called love can bring!"
As she starts to fade away from life; suddenly, so suddenly........ ....a telephone ring.

The Rose of Innocence

As I wander through the field, I feel a longing
deep inside.
I stand and stare into the sky. At what point did I
die inside?
There was a time when I would lie in a field... a
lot?
One by one a petal would fall, as I say the words
"she loves me? She loves me not?

At what age that was I do not know.
It seems so long, so long ago.
I used to watch nature at play, now I don't have the
time of day.

I felt so carefree, happy, reborn.
I'd smell the roses, despite the thorns.
That part of me now, seems so hollow.
The taste of happiness is so hard to swallow.

If there was a tree or a mountain to climb, I'd be
there. It was so sublime.
I used to watch a butterfly in flight.
It'd flutter, and sputter, then go out of sight.

Now, it seems, things come and go.
If a butterfly flies by, I can't tell you so.

I work a lot now, and don't "have time" for such things.
I can no longer look at the butterfly or its wings.

How does one outgrow?
The feelings you get at the first sign of snow.
It is the time of snowball fights, and riding the sled.
At what point in my life did I suddenly get misled?

I've let life slip by me now without a glance.
I can only wonder if I'll get a second chance.
With pain-filled rage I get a sense, that somebody came along and stole my innocence!

Standing in the field; so scared and alone,
with tears in my eyes, I let out a moan.
As tears fall, I know what I must do.
I lie in the grass, still wet with dew.

Closing my eyes, I reach for what I forgot.
The petals fall to the ground and I say "She loves me? She loves me not?" I realize now that it's not too late to feel reborn.
I smell the rose; I smile when I get pricked by the thorn.

The Tyrant

The first week we met you, you were Mr. Nice.

Before long, your true colors came out, your heart was cold as ice.

You hit us without bruising us, by hitting the soft spot on the top of our head.

The first time I saw you hit my MOM, I wanted you DEAD.

You came into our lives and brought us such great turmoil.

If to be like you; you wanted me, that plan I did foil.

It is your influence that has helped me shape my life.

I know how to raise my kid, and how to respect my wife.

You made sure to count, measure, and organize the food in the house.

You would wait and see if we had a snack, then trap us like a mouse.

Let's not stop at just the food, hey here's an idea.

Let's have us only take a bath once a week, only 52 times a year.

That way the kids can laugh at us; when teachers tell us to wash our hands.

That ridicule was not enough, there was more that you had planned.

You decided to put us down in belittlement, telling us “You won't amount to much".

But here I am finally a man. Your cold cruelty came close, but my heart it did not touch.

I have so many memories of how evil a man you are.

You have caused pain and suffering; my mind still has the scar.

I remember the day that I stood up to you, and glared right into your eyes.

You got so mad; you couldn't believe that I would dare defy.

There was that look in your eye the day that you

did gloat; when my brother, while you cut his hair,

had to hold a knife to his throat.

You tried so many things to beat me down, but they never worked.

My strength, integrity, stubbornness, and perseverance I never shirked.

You see you were a tyrant, and I will never forget.

How you and my mom had everything, all we got

was neglect. I have fought you all my life, and

always I have been true, you never beat me down,

was that the best that you could do?

I see right through you, and of your facades.

You are nothing but a COWARD, and a lion without claws. It is your example that has given me due cause, to do just the opposite, and learn from all your flaws.

I am done now, but I wanted you to know.
Yes, you were a tyrant, but I withstood your blow.

The Ugly

A Victims Love...

I think about the past and all those memories.

There were good times, fun times, and also miseries.

I broke into a nervous sweat; my heat beat faster.

As I reach for the phone, I remember our laughter.

We were, friends, family and enemies.....

Sometimes at night I thought “not tonight please!"

I gained my strength from my only friend, God

above.

Why did you taint and twist, our love?

We were so close, we would fight, or even die for one another.

Why was your warped kind of love, hidden from Mother?

I hold back the tears and dial his number.

Thinking back at it now, I couldn't have been
much dumber.

"We need to talk about the past, and what you did"

I say boldly; the first act of courage ever to him
that I ever did.

"I'm sorry for hurting you" was your response.

"YES!" I think, my heart leaps for joy...... for once.

"We need to talk face to face" I get bolder.

"Sure, no problem" from him barely older.

With shaky hands I hang up the phone.

Tears of confirmation flood my every bone.

It was later that week that reality set in.

I was so shocked; I don't know where to begin.

There we were face to face.

I was finally a member of the human race.

I don't remember what it was that I said at first.
But his first words to me were "I don't remember any of it!" my heart burst.
"COWARD!" I scream inside my head.
His words made me wish I were dead.

"I'm supposed to be the one that should forget.
You did sick things to me and face to face you
FORGET" The knife to the heart was more than I
could take.
He tried to comfort me with a hug.   What a fake.

What am I to do now?
Pretend it was a dream, it'll all get better somehow.
I tell him "You need help"
A shrug of his shoulders shows how he felt.

He goes into a conversation like "all is good" I feel
sick, hollow, my heart splinters like wood.
I cursed myself over and over that day.

"That was stupid! Naive! It'll never be o.k.

Now my heart and mind is in a state of confusion. "Is this all real, or just an Illusion?" You are family, my friend, and an enemy too I love you, I hate you, but I forgive you.....

A Victim's Strength

Perhaps you may remember the time when I faced
my molester.

When like a slap to the face, his lies he did fester.
So why is it I am bringing it up today?
Because I was hoping there would be no more
delay.

I get another invite to talk to him once more.
"PLEASE! PLEASE! Let the truth come out" in
my mind I implore.
As smart as I am I still find it so hard to believe.
"This time things will be different!" Why am I
still so NAIVE!

So here we are again, just having a nice old talk.
First in the car, and then as we walk.
"We have to figure out a solution" I say. "And
resolve this once and for all." "I would like to
admit to it, but I don't remember any of it at all."

Here we are going round and round right where we
finished.

I had hoped for something different; but that hope had diminished.
"You're not one to make up stories" he continued at last.
"But I really don't remember, that part of the past."

And then there was a pause, and the sound of dead air.
Then I knew I was being stupid. My molester did not care.
His next statement made we want to scream.
"Are you sure that all wasn't just some kind of dream?"

Again, my feelings of rage and being crushed tried to overtake me.
"You take my soul, and my innocence and you can't admit you raped me!" These thoughts want to come out; but it would be of no avail. My fists want to hit him. To just flail and flail.

As quick as lightning we had resumed a normal conversation. I then realized why it was he really arranged for us to speak.
He was hoping to sway me, make me retract my statement, make me WEAK!

But I won again you son-of-a-B.
You will never, ever again overpower ME!

I am sure that we will have this encounter again.
With my sanity intact, and my friends at my back,
I will always WIN!

The Intruder

I sit down thinking about past memories, there's a lot of pain and mixed-up psychologies.

I remember my stomach, doing its topsy-turvy dance as I experience the confusion brought on by circumstance.

The impending knowledge of doom kept me awake with fright, then the intruder would arrive until the late hours of the night.

He would arrive doing a deed that brought him sick pleasure.

I was a prize, a secret, some kind of treasure.

My innocence vanished, sucked into a black hole.

The intruder was a monster, who didn't seem to have a soul.

Why was I the one that he chose?

Only his mixed-up mind really knows.

For years and years, he continued his assault.
All this time I thought I was at fault.

All those years I endured and endured; have taken their effect, I'm still not fully cured.

I lost my self-esteem, innocence, and willpower
My recovery has been slow, but I've improved by the hour.

As I think about the intruder and all that he has done.
I believe that despite his efforts; I have won.

There's a picture of understanding that I begin to see.
The intruder for me, also had one for he.

Maybe it's because of this that I realize his sickness.

I know why he is who he is, and offer the intruder FORGIVENESS.

The Terror in My Mind

I lay in the covers while the fear consumes me.
I know he is coming soon; bringing with him
despair.
My heart beats, a very e-rrat-ic beat.
Then I hear his footsteps approach.

Chorus:
Oh God! I wish I could be blind,
to the terror in my mind.
The terror in my mind,
the terror in my mind.

Quietly, he slips into my bed.
Before long, his hands begin to grope.
I can hardly breathe; he's trying to get inside me.
But I don't let him penetrate too deep.

Chorus:

Oh God! I wish I could be blind,
to the terror in my mind.
The terror in my mind,
to the terror in my mind.

I think, that he is almost done.
My mind prays that it will end soon. I wish I had
the guts to tell him that what he is doing is RAPE!

Chorus:

Oh God! I wish I could be blind,
to the terror in my mind.
The terror in my mind,
the terror in my mind.

Finally, his hands, mouth, and body part are done.
His sick body retreats, I'm still awake.
Soon, he is snoring, and my mind is roaring.
Sleep comes so easily to him.

Chorus:

Oh God! I wish I could be blind,
to the terror in my mind.
The terror in my mind,
the terror in my mind.

I lay awake, not sure what is happening to me.
My soul is gone, I feel so drained.
Fin-al-ly, I can get to sleep.
But by now the sun is coming up.

Chorus:

Oh God! I wish I could be blind,
to the terror in my mind.
The terror in my mind,
the terror in my mind.

I feel so ashamed.
Am I to blame?
I go about the day, trying to escape my haze.

'Cause I know, tonight he will be back.

Chorus:

Oh God! I wish I could be blind.

to the terror in my mind.

The terror in my mind,

the terror in my mind........

Isabelle

There was a woman on this Earth that was full of cheer, humor, and love.

In her there was peace she was as gentle as a dove.

To a great deal of people, she meant a lot.

If she were a flower, she'd be a forget-me-not.

When her husband would discipline her kids and send them to their room.

She would be baking her pineapple cookies and graham cracker pie; it would take away their gloom.

Her grandkids would say they love their weekends with her the best.

She treated them all fairly; they can attest.

The weekend line-up consisted of Dukes of Hazzard, Knight Rider, Wheel of Fortune and the Muppet Show.

Why she watched these types of shows with her Grand-kids; only she knew.

Wheel of Fortune brought competition to her eyes

She would guess with the kids. For the winner a dollar was the prize.

A hint from the grandkids brought the Atari into the room.

With them she played Pitfall, Frogger, Pac-Man and Kaboom.

Yes! The weekends at Nana were certainly fun.

That's what made her number one.

Angel on Earth

You were such an amazing angel when you were here on Earth.

Gracing us with your beauty; sense of humor; and kindness since birth.

Now you are in heaven surrounded by all its spiritual glory.

You are doing the same thing there, because that is your story.

On day 1 we saw your angelic image in the shape of cloud,

It gave us some piece amidst our hearts sad shroud.

On day 2 we saw the rainbow in multiple skies; we began to realize,

Judy! Heaven's newest angel was making her presence known before our very eyes.

You were always quick with a joke, a laugh, or for anyone go the extra mile.

I don't think you realized how quickly you touched people's hearts, with your graciousness, love and smile.

A person like you rarely exists, among the human race.

You will never, ever in our hearts be replaced.

To us our sweet angel you were known as daughter, sister, mom, aunt, grandma, grammy, great grammy, Judy and "My Love". To another you were known as "Judy Puddy"

To which your response was "Ardy Pardy"

No matter what you mean to each one of us we know you loved us with all your heart and miss you very much.

You were the strongest woman/mom that I ever knew.

The lengths you went to protect us boys, not many others would do.

In your honor we should eat corn beef, and think of you smiling over us as we sleep in bed.

As we cry tears of sadness at the thought of you not being here anymore.

Just know Mom! You have touched so many lives, we will all love you forever more.

This is a poem I wrote and read at my 6-month-old boy's memorial service. He is forever in my heart.

Baby Isaac

You came into our lives like an angel straight to heaven; Bringing joy, love, and smiles twenty-four seven.

We were so proud of you at how quick you grew.
You had two teeth-ers, were holding your own bottle, and crawling before we knew.

You always grinned at us when with "stinky winkies" your diaper was filled. You zoomed around our house so confident, at ease, and strong willed.

You were so smart you knew how to use your smile and your charms. You said "pick me up" when you looked at us with very opened arms.

You were a little billy-goat because you tried to climb over our shoulders, and anything else at any opportunity.
Your chair, the toys and Tyler's pictures were your chew victims; you had a wide variety.

Just like a little puppy you chewed and drooled, and drooled and chewed.

You were so cute opening your mouth wide at the airplane sound when we were giving you starter food.

Sweet baby your smile was so infectious it melted our very souls, Warming up all our hearts like fiery hot coals.

We nicknamed you "Mister-Mister, Fussle-butt, Chompers, Curious George, Billy-goat, and Ike." You were so adorable and perfect that everyone who knew you; did like.

To the baby sitter you grinned at them and gave them a surprise. A wonderful golden shower; you were aiming for their eyes.

When we talked to you would hit your legs in excitement and grinned from ear to ear. And as you learned each new task you did it without any fear.

When it came time to change your diaper there was a lesson you wanted me to learn. How to change your diaper while you did a 180-degree turn?

Isaac wonderful Isaac, your smell was innocent and pure it will remain ingrained into our senses for eternity, I'm sure.

We chuckled at you whenever you sucked on your big toe.

In your place up there in heaven they're laughing already; we know.

You always seemed to know that special time to puke, On Grandma's shirt, or at your dedication ceremony, I am sure it was not a fluke.

You loved your big brother and played with him with sheer delight. You smiled at everyone you saw, like a ray of heavenly light.

We don't know the reason why God took you from us in such a short period of time. Maybe heaven needed you more, to help the angels shine.

You were always extremely happy it was contagious and it enveloped everyone around. It surrounded them, embraced them and filled them with happiness abound.

You'll be so missed here on Earth it's you we all did love. I hope that you smile at us while you are above.

When God took you from us, we felt terrified, sucked into a dark hole. Like a vortex we felt trapped, our lives were spinning out of control.

We wish you were still here with us, as our hearts have been thoroughly crushed. But God has taken you into his hands; your face; his fingers have brushed.

So gently, he will care for you, and place you with the angels that he trusts. When we die, you will run to us for your memory never rusts.

As you took your ride on an angel's wings with the wind blowing through your curl; I'm sure you giggled and smiled and made the angel's happiness unfurl.

We had visions of the wonderful boy that we knew that you would be. We will miss you and love you for all eternity.

We love you and miss you Isaac, thank you for blessing us with the best six months of our lives.

Chess helped me through a lot of my childhood. Here is a picture I was given by my wife to represent me.

The artist is a friend of ours. Thank you for reading my writings.

Mark Greenlaw

CPSIA information can be obtained
at www.ICGtesting.com
Printed in the USA
LVHW060952270922
729388LV00006B/41

9 780123 456823